LOST TRAMWAYS OF IRELAND BELFAST

PETER WALLER

GRAFFEG

CONTENTS

Introduction	3
Pre-electric era	15
The early electric era	17
Depots	20
City Centre	21
Bridge End	30
Albert Bridge	31
Glengormley route	34
York Road Station	39
Greencastle	40
Queen's Quay Station	41
Queen's Road	43
Dundonald route	44
Bloomfield	45
Ormeau Road	46
Stranmillis	47
Malone Road route	48
Balmoral route	51
Donegall Road route	53
Springfield	54
Ballygomartin	56
Ligoniel route	59
Cliftonville	62
Ex-Cavehill & Whitewell	63

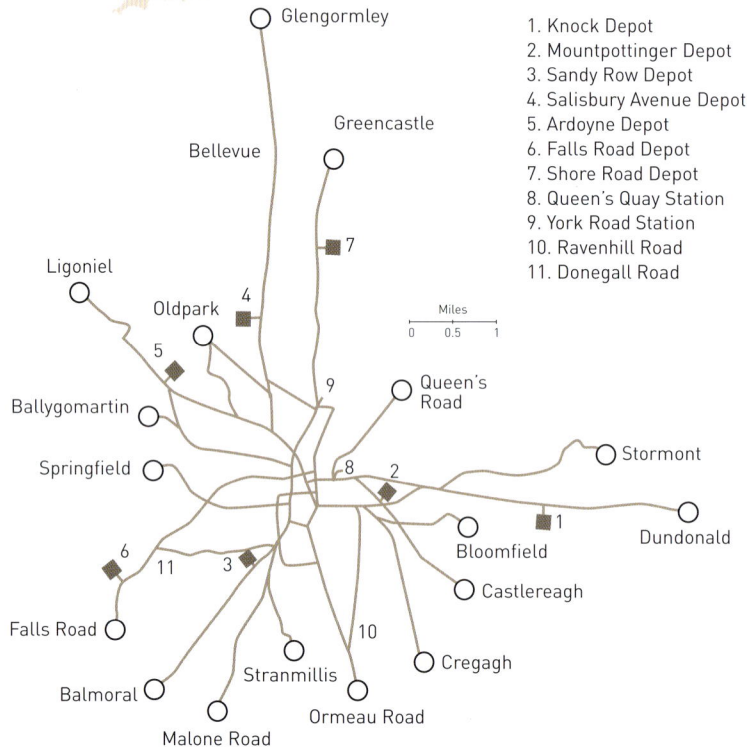

BELFAST

1. Knock Depot
2. Mountpottinger Depot
3. Sandy Row Depot
4. Salisbury Avenue Depot
5. Ardoyne Depot
6. Falls Road Depot
7. Shore Road Depot
8. Queen's Quay Station
9. York Road Station
10. Ravenhill Road
11. Donegall Road

Glengormley
Greencastle
Bellevue
Ligoniel
Oldpark
Ballygomartin
Springfield
Queen's Road
Stormont
Bloomfield
Dundonald
Castlereagh
Falls Road
Cregagh
Balmoral
Stranmillis
Ormeau Road
Malone Road

Miles
0   0.5   1

INTRODUCTION

Tramway legislation in Ireland predated that within Great Britain. The relevant legislation was enshrined in two Acts: the Tramways (Ireland) Act of 1860 and the Tramways (Ireland) Amendment Act of the following year. The Acts empowered local authorities to grant licences to companies to operate tramways for a 21-year period. It was not until 1870 that Great Britain saw the Royal Assent given to the Tramways Act. The licensee could construct the tramway itself or the route could be constructed by the local authority and leased as part of the franchise to the operator. Initially, it was expected that private companies would always operate the tramways built; however, in 1883, Huddersfield Corporation in the West Riding of Yorkshire, having constructed a new steam tramway to serve the town, was unable to find a licensee willing to take on operation and so became the first municipal operator of trams within the British Isles.

The earlier Acts imposed a number of restrictions upon the tramway builder and operator; with the benefit of hindsight, it can be seen that these had a negative impact upon tramway development in the United Kingdom and undoubtedly represented one factor in the demise of the tramcar from the 1920s onwards. One of these clauses in Belfast required the builder and operator of the tramway to maintain the public highway to a distance of two feet outside each running line; this effectively made the tramway owner responsible for the upkeep of the road surface on those streets where trams operated. At a time when the condition of the public highway was often poor, the well-built and well-maintained section over which the trams operated became a magnet for other road users. As road traffic increased, so trams – despite the fact that the road had been constructed to accommodate them – were increasingly perceived as a cause of road traffic delays.

The second weakness within the legislation was the so-called 'scrap iron clause'; this permitted the licensor – usually the local authority – to take over the assets (such as the trams) owned by the licensee at asset value – including depreciation – rather than reflecting the value of the business. As a result, tramway licensees became increasingly unwilling to invest in their business as the licence period came towards its end. The Act permitted the termination of the licence after 21 years and every seven years thereafter. For company-owned operations this sword of Damocles meant that the threat of municipalisation was ever present and, even if never exercised, was sufficient to ensure that modernisation might never take place. The classic example here is the tramways of Bristol; operated throughout their career by a company but with the constant threat of takeover by Bristol Corporation, the system survived through until 1941 operating open-top and unvestibuled trams that would not have been out of place on the first electric tramways built at the end of the 19th century whereas other systems were operating state-of-the-art modern trams by World War II.

This volume is the first of the series to cover the tramways of Ireland.

The horse tram era

The Belfast Tramways Co was first promoted in early 1871 and, on 22 December 1871, the company obtained powers to construct a network of horse tramways to serve the city. A small network of 5ft 3in routes was authorised; these linked the centre with Botanic Gardens, Clifton Street, York Road railway station, Corporation Street and Ormeau Bridge. Work started on construction in early 1872 and the first – German-built – horse trams were officially launched on 28 August 1872; by this date, following an Act of 10 August 1872, the original company was replaced by the Belfast Street Tramways Co.

Further Acts followed to permit the construction of extensions and, in 1878, a further Act was obtained to permit the conversion of the system from 5ft 3in to 4ft 8½in. In applying for this power, the company had also sought powers to operate steam trams – having successfully experimented with steam traction the previous year – but this was rejected due to opposition from Lord Redesdale.

Over the next two decades the company continued to expand the network, with the last extensions being authorised in 1899. These last routes to be completed included the lines to Knock along Newtownards Road and Upper Newtownards Road, to Stranmillis, along Malone Road, Ravenhill Road, Cliftonville Road and along

Grosvenor Road to Springfield.

In addition to Belfast Street Tramways, there were also three other horse tram lines in the city, two of which ultimately became subsidiaries of Belfast Street Tramways, which were promoted by other companies but operated by the Belfast Street Tramways. The first of these two lines was the Sydenham District Tramways Co, which constructed a route from Holywood Arches to Belmont; this line opened in 1889 and was to pass to the Street Tramways Co in August 1902. The second of these operators was the Belfast & Ligoniel Tramway, which constructed a line from Brookfield Street to St Mark's Church in Ligoniel; this route opened on 24 April 1893 and was also to pass to the Street Tramways Co in August 1902. The third was a short 110yd link into Queen's Quay station that was promoted by the Belfast & County Down Railway; this was to pass directly to Belfast Corporation on 1 January 1905.

The corporation takes over

With the completion of the final extensions, the horse tramway network had reached its maximum extent – almost 25 route miles – and was operated by 171 horse trams. However, in early 1902 the corporation gave the Street Tramways Co notice that powers to purchase the tramway compulsorily were to be sought. Although this was initially opposed, eventually terms were agreed and the powers formally enshrined into an Act – the Belfast Corporation (Tramways) Act – passed in mid-1904. On 1 January 1905, the corporation took over ownership and operation of the system. Alongside the track and trams, the corporation also acquired the company's depots: Antrim Road, Knock, Lisburn Road, Mountpottinger and Sandy Row (where the main workshops were situated).

One reason for the acquisition was the corporation's desire to see the network electrified and, during 1905, work proceeded rapidly on the conversion of the existing network. In order to operate the newly electrified system, Loughborough-based Brush was contracted to produce 170 open-top cars (Nos 1-170); these were all equipped with Brill-type 21E four-wheel trucks. In addition, it was also decided to rebuild a number of horse cars – five initially, but eventually a total of 50 – into electric trams (Nos 201-50); Brush was again contracted to supply equipment to allow the conversion, including the four-wheel trucks.

Work on electrification was rapid, with the result that the first electric trams – on the routes to Malone Road, Ormeau Road, Springfield Road and Stranmillis – commenced operation on 30 November 1905, with all of the other ex-horse tram routes following on 5 December 1905.

The system expands

The final extension completed under the 1904 Act – that to Queen's Road – was opened on 11 August 1908. The existing fleet was supplemented by the construction of a further 22 'Standard' cars – Nos 171-92 – between 1908 and 1910. Although again Brush supplied the equipment – including the four-wheel trucks – the corporation constructed the open-balcony bodies itself at Sandy Row Works. These were the first Belfast trams to be completed with top covers; by the date of their construction, similar open top covers were gradually being fitted to the older cars.

The next expansion to the system saw the corporation takeover the operation of the Cavehill & Whitewell route from Chichester Park to Glengormley on 2 June 1911. The corporation also acquired eight of the company's 10 trams; these were to become Nos 193-200 and – with one

exception – all were eventually rebuilt to appear similar to the corporation's 'Standard' cars.

By the end of the first decade of the 20th century pressure for further extensions grew as the city developed. Proposals in 1909 resulted in the construction of a number of new routes and extensions – from St Mark's Church to Ligoniel, to Bloomfield, to Houston Park at Castlereagh, a link along Ravenhill Road from South Parade to Rosetta, from Ridgeway Street to Stranmillis, along Botanic Avenue (to provide a connection between the Ormeau Road route and Shaftesbury Square), along Donegall Road (to a junction with the existing Falls Road route) and from Crumlin Road along Oldpark Road to connect into the existing route along Cliftonville Road – that were all to commence operation on 29 January 1913. The opening of the Botanic Avenue section permitted the closure of the line along Ormeau Avenue – the first abandonment of any electric route in the city.

In order to operate these new services, a further batch of 41 open-balcony cars – Nos 251-91 – was constructed at Sandy Row between 1913 and 1919. The acquisition of these cars along with the completion of the extensions opened in 1913 marked the final major changes undertaken under the aegis of Andrew Nance; he had first joined the Belfast Street Tramways in 1881 and had been the corporation's first general manager. Following his retirement in 1916, he was succeeded later in the year by James Moffett.

Post-war and the 1920s

After World War I and the troubles associated with the creation of the Irish Free State and Northern Ireland, in which the trams suffered some damage and some services were temporarily withdrawn as a result of civil unrest, a new general manager, Samuel Carlisle, was appointed in October 1922 to replace James Moffett.

The early 1920s were to witness the final expansion of the tramway network. In September 1923 the Belmont route was extended to the gates at Stormont, on 7 July 1924 the Knock route was extended by two-thirds of a mile to Dundonald and on 18 December 1924 the section along Chichester Street in the city centre was opened. The final extension to the system occurred on 23 July 1925 with the opening of the branch off Shankill Road to serve Ballygomartin. This took

the system to its maximum extent – almost 51½ route miles. In order to operate the fleet, the corporation employed 341 electric trams; of these the vast majority were the 'Standard Reds', but the fleet also included eight cars – Nos 193-200 – that had been acquired following the takeover of the Cavehill & Whitwell as well as the 50 fully enclosed 'Moffett' cars – No 292-341 – that were delivered during late 1920 and 1921.

Carlisle's years as general manager were not easy. In 1926 the corporation decided – despite opposition – to introduce bus services, with the first route being introduced on 4 October 1926. More significantly, the Motor Vehicles (Traffic and Regulations) Act of 1926, which came into force the following year, eventually resulted in the so-called 'Bus Wars' between June and December 1928 when, due to the lack of new by-laws, unrestricted competition was permitted between bus operators and corporation tram services, with the former undercutting the fares on the latter. This and other problems made Carlisle's position increasingly difficult and he was effectively made the scapegoat for the deteriorating financial position, being replaced by the general manager of Leeds Corporation Tramways, William Chamberlain, who took over in October 1928.

The 1930s

Chamberlain's first role was to re-establish the tramway network as a robust operator. This was to be achieved by the acquisition of 50 new trams – the first 40, Nos 342-91, were supplied by Brush with locally based Service Motor Works supplying the final 10; all were fitted with Maley & Taunton 8ft 0in wheelbase swinglink four-wheel trucks – along with the rebuilding as fully enclosed of a number of the 'Standard Reds'. In order to highlight the new era, the new trams plus those rebuilt were to emerge in a new blue livery.

Chamberlain was not to be general manger for long; he departed in 1931 to be replaced by Robert McCreary, but he had put the tramways into a much better position than when he first took over. It was the new general manager who set the specification for the next batch of trams – Nos 392-441 – that were built by English Electric and Service Motor Works. These streamlined cars, all equipped again with Maley & Taunton 8ft 0in wheelbase swinglink four-wheel trucks, were destined to be the last new trams acquired by the tramway. These entered service during 1935 and 1936.

On 1 October 1936 the first tramway abandonment since 1913 occurred, with the replacement of the outer section of the Cregagh route beyond the original terminus and Gibson Park as a result of the poor state of the track. The same reason resulted in the diversion of the Castlereagh trams from Mountpottinger Road to operate via Albert Bridge in August 1936, although the bulk of track remained in situ in order to provide access to Mountpottinger depot.

Although these losses were not significant, they were indicative that – despite the recent acquisition of the 'McCreary' cars – there were doubts over the future of the tramway. In October 1936, following powers obtained in the Belfast Corporation Act of 1930, the transport committee decided to experiment with the introduction of trolleybuses. The route selected for conversion was that along the Falls Road and this was to become trolleybus operated from 28 March 1938. The Falls Road depot was closed to trams at the same time.

The trolleybus experiment was to prove a success and, in January 1939, the decision was made that the entire tramway system was to be converted to bus and trolleybus operation over the next five years. However, events in Poland later that year were to result in these plans going awry.

World War II

As elsewhere, the declaration of war in September 1939 resulted in some immediate changes. To passengers, the most obvious would have been the painting of the collision fenders to white, in order to improve visibility during the blackout; this also resulted in white bands being painted on traction columns. In order to reduce further visible light, headlamps were all fitted with shields. Although Belfast – as with other major cities and industrial centres – was to be a target for the Luftwaffe, unlike other operators Belfast's tram network was to escape relatively lightly. Only one depot – Antrim Road on the night of 15/16 April 1941 – was to suffer significant damage as a result of bombing and, although a number of trams were damaged, none were withdrawn as a result of damage during the war.

Although wartime conditions precluded the planned conversion of the entire system by the middle of the decade, there were a number of tram-to-bus or trolleybus conversions during the period. The first of these occurred on 5 September 1940 when the Ormeau Road via Ravenhill Road service was converted to bus. Two routes – to

Cregagh on 13 February and to Castlereagh via Albert Bridge on 5 June – were converted to trolleybus operation during 1941, with two more – Stormont on 26 March and Dundonald Road (via Queen's Bridge) on 16 November – following in 1942. The second route to Dundonald – via Albert Bridge – was converted to trolleybus operation on 8 March 1943.

The final abandonment to occur during the war occurred on 5 January 1945 when the Ormeau Road via Botanic Avenue service – route 16 – was suspended as a result of urgent sewer repairs in Botanic Avenue; although the 16 was rerouted to operate via Cromac Street to supplement the 15, trams were never restored to the Botanic Avenue section.

The post-war years

If war had not intervened the Belfast system would have been converted to bus or trolleybus operation by 1945; delays in the delivery of new trolleybuses meant, however, that much of the system – particularly west of the Lagan – was still tram operated. The policy remained, nonetheless, one of conversion, but, in the era of post-war austerity, this was to take nearly a decade.

It was not until 6 May 1946 – when the Bloomfield route (20) was converted to trolleybus operation – that the system further contracted. The next year was to witness two conversions: on 21 April buses replaced trams on routes 37 and 38 to Donegall Road whilst on 31 August the Cliftonville route (14) was also converted to bus operation.

On 19 April 1948 the routes to Ormeau Road via Cromac Street – the 15 and 16 – were converted to trolleybus operation. Despite these closures, which had reduced the system to about half its maximum size, the tramways still carried about half of the 257 million passengers carried that year; 1948 was to be the peak year for the numbers transported by Belfast Corporation.

There was to be only one conversion during 1949; this was, however, the long route northwards to Glengormley, of which the section north of Chichester Park represented the line operated by the Cavehill & Whitwell Tramway prior to the corporation's takeover on 2 June 1911. The Glengormley section – routes 1 and 2 that terminated at Chichester Park, the 4 to Bellevue and the 3 and 5 to Glengormley itself – was converted to trolleybus operation on 24 January. This closure also resulted in the closure of the depot at Salisbury Avenue to trams. Also casualties during 1949 were the last surviving rebuilt horse trams that had been converted to electric traction in 1905. Nos 213/44/49/50 had been retained latterly for works duties and No 249 was retained for preservation; it made one final appearance – in 1953 – during a tour organised by the Light Railway Transport League to permit photographs to be taken prior to the system's final conversion. It is now preserved at Cultra.

Into the 1950s

Following the conversion of the route to Glengormley, there was to be a pause of more than a year before the next tram routes were to succumb. On 21 August 1950 the service into the siding at York Road station – the Northern Counties Committee station – served via York Street was abandoned. The Stranmillis route (27), which had previously terminated at Corporation Street alongside the station, was subsequently linked to Queen's Road, operating via High Street rather than along Chichester Street. This conversion was followed on 1 October 1950 by the conversion of the Greencastle section to Shore Road and route 7 through to Greencastle itself; this was the final tram-to-trolleybus conversion undertaken; thereafter, the remaining routes were all converted to bus and were dependent upon the availability of new (or second-hand) buses. The section as far as Fortwilliam Shore Road, however, remained operational until 3 July 1953 – or earlier – for peak hour services to and from Queen's Road. The acquisition of 11 second-hand trolleybuses from Wolverhampton in 1952 facilitated the end of this tram working.

The early part of 1951 witnessed a wholesale reorganisation of route numbers; the surviving tram routes were all allocated numbers within the range 50-69. Three routes were to be converted to bus operation during 1951; these were the services to Oldpark Road on 30 April, to Stranmillis on 29 July and Malone Road on 4 November. The closures of 1951 also permitted the closure of a further depot – Shore Road – to trams. This left two remaining depots – Ardoyne and Mountpottinger – that were to remain operational until the final closure in 1954.

The ongoing problems in the supply of replacement buses led to no further reduction to the tram network until late in 1952. On 10 November three sections – the routes to Balmoral, Ballygomartin and Springfield – were all converted to bus operation; as with the earlier conversion of the Greencastle route, the sections along the Balmoral and Springfield routes to Windsor Park and Mackie's Foundry were retained for peak hour only services. With the greater availability of buses, these peak hour services were themselves to cease on 3 July 1953.

The final year

The start of 1953 saw the Belfast system reduced to three routes – to Ligoniel (via Crumlin Road or via Shankill Road) and to Queen's Road – with the three sections – to Fortwilliam Shore Road, Mackie's Foundry and Windsor Park – that were used by peak hour services only.

In order to alleviate the problem in obtaining sufficient replacement buses, the corporation acquired 100 buses second-hand from London Transport. These first appeared on the Crumlin Road section in February 1953 and their greater availability resulted in the number of operational trams being reduced progressively. Following the end of the peak hour only services in July 1953, all day services on the surviving routes ceased on 12 October 1953; thereafter, any operation was limited to peak hour services only and these were progressively reduced as additional buses became available. The spur into Queen's Quay station was last used on 30 October 1953.

By early 1954, the increased availability of buses meant that no trams were operational and, on 28 February 1954, the official closure of the system took place with a procession of 12 cars headed from Queen's Road to Ardoyne depot via Shankill Road. The last tram in the procession was 'Chamberlain' No 389.

Of the tram fleet, the vast majority were scrapped. Apart from the rebuilt horse car No 249, only one other electric tram – 'Chamberlain' No 357 – was preserved; like No 249, this is also now on display at Cultra. In addition to these trams, Cultra is also home to the only surviving Belfast Street Tramways Co horse tram, No 118.

Cavehill & Whitewell Tramway

Authorised by the Cavehill & Whitewell Tramways Order of 1881, the three-mile standard gauge tramway ran from the terminus of the Belfast Street Tramways at Chichester Park Gate through to the Glengormley Arms. When first opened on 1 July 1882, the service was provided by steam trams with trailers but these proved inefficient and so, from 1896, horse trams were operated. Following a contract with British Electric Traction, the route was electrified, with the new service being introduced on 12 February 1906. In order to run the electric service, 10 open-top trams were supplied by Brush of Loughborough. On 2 June 1911, as a result of an agreement made

the previous year, the corporation took over the assets of the company. Of the 10 trams, eight entered service with the new owners, the other two having been sold in 1909 to Mansfield & District Light Railways in England. The company's route remained tram operated until conversion on 23 January 1949.

A note on the photographs

The majority of the illustrations in this book have been drawn from the collection of the Online Transport Archive, a UK-registered charity that was set up to accommodate collections put together by transport enthusiasts who wished to see their precious images secured for the long-term. Further information about the archive can be found at: www.onlinetransportarchive.org or email secretary@onlinetransportarchive.org.

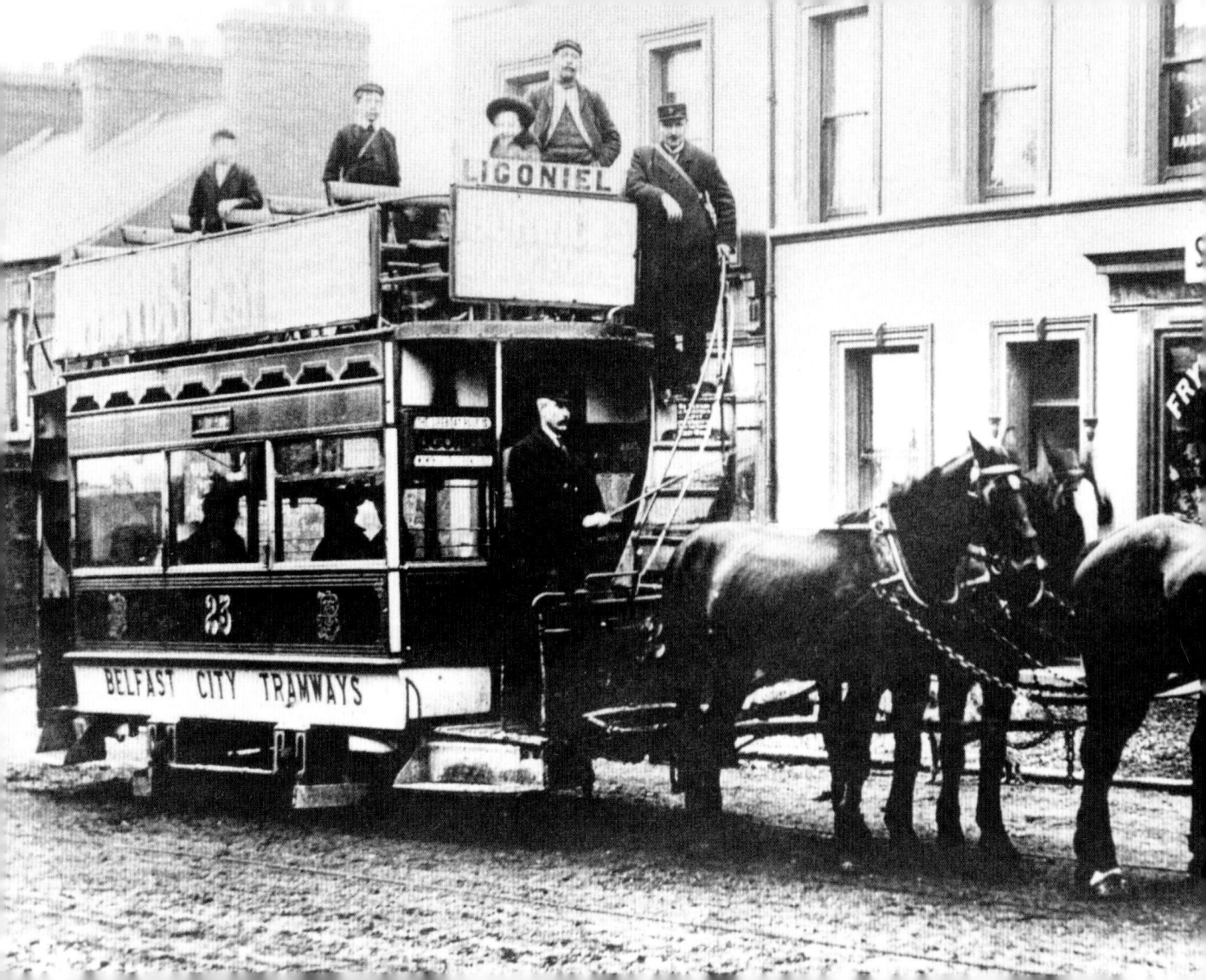

PRE-ELECTRIC ERA

As a result of powers obtained on 22 December 1871, the first horse tramway service in Belfast was introduced on 28 August 1872 between Castle Place and Botanic Gardens. This was soon followed by additional routes; these early lines were all constructed to a gauge of 5ft 3in but later in the 1870s powers were obtained to convert the system to 4ft 8½in (in reality the actual gauge finally adopted was 4ft 9in). The network of horse tramways operated by the Belfast Street Tramways grew over the succeeding decades and by, 1 January 1905, when the assets of the company were acquired by the corporation, the system extended over almost 25 route miles. When the corporation took over, it acquired a fleet of 171 horse trams. No 23 is pictured here in the livery of the Belfast City Tramways.

THE EARLY ELECTRIC ERA

Following its purchase of the assets of the Belfast Street Tramways under the powers of the Belfast Corporation (Tramways) Act of 1904, the corporation undertook the rapid conversion of the existing horse tramway network with the result that all of the ex-horse routes were electrified by 5 December 1905 with the exception of the Durham Street route, which was never to be converted. Of all the major cities within the British Isles, Belfast was amongst the last to see the conversion from horse to electric trams. In order to operate the new system, the corporation purchased 170 open-top cars from Brush; Nos 1-170 were all equipped with Brill 21E four-wheel trucks but, by the date of their introduction, open-top cars were already starting to become dated. As a result, from 1907 work commenced on equipping the trams with open-balcony top covers; the work was completed in 1920. This view on Royal Avenue sees two of this first batch of trams approaching the Royal Avenue Hotel, still in their original open-top condition.

A busy view of High Street with the Albert Memorial in the background sees at least seven trams plying their trade amongst all of the other road users. All the trams have been fitted with open-balcony top covers but their platforms remain open to the elements. Although undated, the lack of any of the fully enclosed 'Moffett' cars – dating to late 1920 and early 1921 – would suggest a date in the period immediately after World War I. Note the very short – and unusual – top cover on the tram nearest the camera. The Albert Memorial Clock, situated in Queen's Square, was constructed between 1865 and 1869 to the designs of William Joseph Barre. As a consequence of its construction on marshy land using wooden piles, the tower tilts in one direction and is about four feet off the perpendicular at its top. As a result, the structure was modified in 1924 with the loss of some decorative work. The structure has undergone a major restoration project, with work being completed in 2002.

DEPOTS

Mountpottinger depot was one of six inherited by the corporation from the Belfast Street Tramways Co; all were converted for the use of electric trams except Lisburn Road. A somewhat constrained site, the depot possessed 17 parallel under cover roads along with a repair shop accessed by a short connection off Mountpottinger Road. This view, taken on the occasion of an enthusiasts' tour of the depot on 6 June 1953, sees 'Chamberlain' No 364 alongside two of the 'McCreary' type, Nos 405 and 441. The latter was the highest numbered tram to operate in the city. The spur heading off to the left in front of the gate gave access to the Madrid Street Permanent Way Yard. Mountpottinger was one of two depots – the other being Ardoyne – that were still operational when the final trams operated.

Castle Junction – the intersection of Royal Avenue, Castle Place, Donegall Place and Castle Street – was very much the central focus of the tramway system and here 'McCreary' No 429 is heading northbound into Royal Avenue in August 1951 shortly after the surviving tramway services were renumbered in the 50-69 number range. The 50 'McCreary' cars – named after the then general manager Robert McCreary – were the last new trams acquired by the corporation. The first of the batch – No 392 – was constructed in England by English Electric, as were Nos 423-41, with the remaining 30 – Nos 393-422 – being constructed locally by Service Motor Works; all were equipped with Maley & Taunton 8ft 0in wheelbase four-wheel trucks and were delivered during 1935 and 1936.

Overlooked by the statue of Henry Cooke (a leading clergyman of the mid-19th century) in front of the Royal Belfast Academical Institution, two 'McCreary' cars pass on the curve between College Square and Wellington Place in August 1953. Founded in 1814 and given its royal title in 1831, the Royal Belfast Academical Institution or 'Inst', as it is nicknamed locally, is an independent boys' grammar school. Its building – the façade of which can be seen behind the two trams – was designed by Sir John Soane, better known as the architect of the Bank of England in London, with construction starting in 1810. By the date of the photograph, the city centre terminus of the Ligoniel route was in Fisherwick Place (just around the corner from this angle), where a crossover existed, in order to avoid congestion through reversing at Castle Junction. The blind on No 418, heading towards the terminus, has already been altered for its next outbound trip.

In August 1953, with the neo-classical Scottish Provident Institution building behind it, 'McCreary' No 398 is pictured turning left from the north side of Donegall Square into Donegall Place with an outbound service on route 56 towards Ligoniel. In the background, a trolleybus on route 7 to Greencastle can be seen emerging from Wellington Place. The Scottish Provident Institution, situated on Donegall Square West, was constructed between 1897 and 1902 to the design of Robert Young and John Mackenzie. The central bay, which is bowed, incorporates four panels that portray the trades – printing, rope-making, shipbuilding and weaving – that dominated the local economy at the start of the 20th century. The Grade A listed building was extensively renovated about a decade ago.

Pictured in front of the Great Victoria Street terminus of the Great Northern Railway (Ireland) in August 1951 is 'McCreary' No 428 with a service towards Malone Road. The driver is looking over his shoulder, presumably waiting for the signal from the conductor that all those wishing to alight or board had done so. The original station – built on the site of a linen mill – was opened courtesy of the Ulster Railway on 12 August 1839 but the station illustrated here was completed in 1848; it was designed by John Godwin, the Ulster Railway's engineer. It became the terminus of the GNR(I) in 1876, when the Ulster Railway merged with two other railways and the newly-enlarged company adopted the Great Northern name. Much of the station building, including the superb porte-cochère, was demolished in 1968 to permit construction of the Europa Hotel with the remainder following in 1976, when the station finally closed with the opening of Belfast Central station. A new station serving Great Victoria Street opened in September 1995.

With the 40-metre tower of the Assembly Hall of the Presbyterian Church of Ireland in the background, 'Moffett' No 297 is seen heading south along Fisherwick Place on route 31 towards Malone Road. The tram will have commenced its journey at Ballygomartin; from the opening of the extension to Ballygomartin in 1925, the services from there – the 30 via Bedford Street and the 31 via Great Victoria Street – ran as cross-city services to Malone Road until the conversion of that section on 4 November 1951. Cars operating towards Ballygomartin showed route number 33 irrespective of which road they took. Following the conversion of the Malone Road route, Ballygomartin services were linked to Springfield for their final year. Of the buildings visible in this view, only the Assembly Hall, which was completed in 1905 and opened by the then Duke of Argyll, plus the red-brick building immediately to its south and The Crown Bar are still extant.

A busy view on Royal Avenue in the early 1930s sees 'Chamberlain' No 371 heading southbound towards Balmoral on route 17 whilst heading northbound are cars on routes 12 to Oldpark Road, 5 to Ligoniel and 10 to Greencastle. On the west side of the road, the scene is dominated by the city's original Grand Central Hotel. This building, which dated to 1893, provided accommodation for many notable visitors over the years, including groups such as the Beatles and the Rolling Stones. In 1972, the building was taken over by the British Army in order to provide additional accommodation for troops, but this role ceased in the late 1980s and the building was subsequently demolished. The site was redeveloped as the CastleCourt shopping centre. Many of the other buildings on the west side of the road have also disappeared, although those to the east have fared better; another survivor is the Art Deco Bank of Ireland building visible in the distance. The building, which was completed in 1930 to the designs of Joseph Vincent Downes and is listed Grade B+, has been vacant since 2005, although, at the time of writing, plans for its redevelopment are under consideration.

Queen's Bridge was used by services to Queen's Road, Stormont, Dundonald and Castlereagh; however, the wartime conversion of all bar the route to Queen's Road to trolleybus operation resulted in the section of track at Bridge End, passing under the Belfast Central Railway, to Mountpottinger depot being retained for solely trams heading to or from the shipyard extras at peak hours. Here 'DK1' rebuild No 164 – the first tram to emerge in the new blue livery when it was returned to service, rebuilt as fully enclosed, in February 1929 – is seen passing under the railway bridge en route to the depot in August 1953. Note the low clearance over the tram.

As a trolleybus heads inbound, 'DK1' rebuild No 255 heads eastbound over Albert Bridge during August 1951 en route towards Mountpottinger depot. By the date of this photograph, no service trams made use of Albert Bridge; the last passenger route to operate over the bridge had been that to Bloomfield, which had been converted on 5 May 1946. No 255 was one of the first of the batch – Nos 251-91 – of open-balcony 'Standard Reds' built at Sandy Row Works between 1913 and 1919. Originally fitted with Brill 21E four-wheel trucks of 6ft 6in wheelbase, the retrucking of the 'Moffett' class resulted in all 41 being refitted with 7ft 6in wheelbase trucks between 1929 and 1932. At the same time, all 41 were rebuilt as fully enclosed. The background of the view is dominated by the East Bridge Street power station; this was the second power station in the city – following on from the smaller example on Chapel Lane – and was opened in 1898. The coal-fired power station was municipally owned and its construction was designed to cater for the needs of the growing city – including the power required to operate the proposed electrified tramways. Following closure, it was demolished in the 1980s, with the site now occupied by the Santander Bank.

The tramway junction at the southern end of Mountpottinger Road with Albert Bridge Road and Castlereagh Road was one of the most complex outside the city centre. Here another 'DK1' rebuild – No 268 – is pictured pulling out of Mountpottinger Road and turning left into Albertbridge Road; it will then make use of the crossover a short distance along the latter before heading back westwards over the junction into the city centre via Albertbridge Road, the curve at Ropeworks Corner and Lower Newtownards Road. In the distance, an outbound service towards Castlereagh on route 31 can be seen. By the date of this photograph – August 1950 – the services along Albertbridge Road to Dundonald and Stormont as well as that along Cregagh Road to Castlereagh had been trolleybus operated for almost a decade and the only trams to use the junction were those heading to or from Mountpottinger depot.

As a trolleybus waits to emerge from Cregagh Road, 'Chamberlain' No 347 heads towards Albert Bridge and the city centre having departed from Mountpottinger depot. Although the tram service to Cregagh was a relatively early casualty – being converted to trolleybus operation on 13 February 1941 – the route to Bloomfield, which operated along Woodstock Road, was the last passenger service to use Albert Bridge until the service was converted to trolleybus operation on 5 May 1946 – the first post-war conversion. Note the disconnected pointwork in the foreground that would once have permitted trams access to and from Woodstock Road.

GLENGORMLEY ROUTE

As a result of the takeover of the Cavehill & Whitewell route, the corporation acquired its most unusual asset – the estate at Bellevue – which was developed (under the aegis of the Transport Department) into zoological gardens in order to try and generate extra traffic for the route. The Transport Department retained ownership of the gardens well after the demise of the tramways, a fact that often led to the operator's senior management being the butt of humour from their colleagues in other operators. Pictured at Bellevue with an inbound service towards Castle Junction on 5 June 1948 is 'Chamberlain' No 368. Beyond Bellevue, the section towards Glengormley was formed of single track with passing loops.

Also seen at Bellevue is open-top ex-horse car No 247. With the electrification of the system in 1905, the decision was made to convert five of the horse cars to electric traction; with work in hand, the quality of the bodies was such that it was decided to convert a further 45. These cars, equipped with four-wheel 5ft 6in wheelbase trucks supplied by Brush, became Nos 201-50. Being smaller than the new electric cars, these could accommodate only 48 seated passengers as opposed to 54 on Nos 1-170. All of the batch were subsequently rebuilt with end canopies and half-turns with all bar No 244-50 being equipped with open-balcony top covers. Nos 244-50 remained open top throughout their careers. Nos 247-50 differed slightly from the remainder and may possibly have been an amalgam of parts from both horse and electric types. The majority of the ex-horse cars were withdrawn by the end of World War II, although 13 of those fitted with open-balcony top covers survived post-war, as did Nos 247-50; a number were converted into works cars later in their lives, including No 249, which, as a snowplough, was set aside following withdrawal in 1949 and was subsequently preserved. It is now on display at Cultra.

Stretching into the country beyond the city boundary, the Glengormley route was the longest on the system. The northernmost section – from Chichester Park to the terminus – was taken over from the Cavehill & Whitewell on 2 June 1911. The outermost section of the route – from Bellevue to Glengormley – remained single track with passing loops right through until the service was converted to trolleybus operation on 23 January 1949. On 5 June 1948 'DK1' rebuild No 269 is pictured at the terminus prior to heading south with an inbound service. Note the unusual and atypical top cover with which the car was equipped. A total of 41 – Nos 251-91 – cars were built by the corporation between 1913 and 1919 and equipped with Brill-type 6ft 6in wheelbase four-wheel trucks supplied by Brush. Following the decision to retruck the 'Moffett' cars, the 51 cars – plus nine older examples – were equipped with the 7ft 6in trucks from the 'Moffetts' between 1929 and 1932. The trams were also rebuilt as fully enclosed at the same time. This work was undertaken either in Sandy Row Works or by the locally based Service Motor Works. All were withdrawn between 1951 and 1954 and were scrapped.

YORK ROAD STATION

As 'Standard Red' No 2 enters the terminal stub at York Road station, 'Chamberlain' No 389 stands on Whitla Street with a service due to head towards Stranmillis in a pre-World War II view. The Whitla Street line was constructed under the 1892 Order in Council. Prior to this date the line was via Corporation Street, Great George's Street and York Street, which was sanctioned under the 1872 Act. There were proposals in 1920, which were never completed, for a short extension from Whitla Street northwards for about half a mile to Milewater Basin that would have paralleled the railway north from York Road. The station had opened originally for the Belfast & Ballymena Railway on 11 April 1848, but the building visible in this view was the result of major rebuilding undertaken during the 1890s to the designs of Sir Charles Lanyon. As a result of the Midland Railway's acquisition of the Belfast & Northern Counties Railway in 1903, ownership of the station passed to the London, Midland & Scottish Railway (Northern Counties Committee – LMSNCC – as shown on the poster) in 1923. In April 1941 the building suffered serious damage as a result of bombing by the Luftwaffe which resulted in the loss of the Midland Hotel – the building on the station side of Whitla Street – along with the cover over the tram terminus. However, trams continued to serve the terminal stub until 21 August 1950. The horse tramway terminating in Whitla Street was one of the sections originally constructed to 5ft 3in and subsequently converted to standard gauge.

GREENCASTLE

On 12 January 1950 the conductor has almost completed the swinging of the trolleypole on 'Moffett' No 299 at Greencastle. Note the trolleybus overhead – this was a portent for the future, as the route was converted to trolleybus operation on 1 October 1950. The new trolleybus service was extended by about three-quarters of a mile beyond the tram terminus. Tram services to Greencastle owed their origins to a horse tram route; this had initially been opened as far as York Road station, with a terminus on Whitla Street, in 1872, with the northern extension to Greencastle via York Road and Shore Road following in the early 1890s.

Two generations of tram – 'McCreary' No 428 of 1936 and 'Moffett' No 330 of 1921 – pass on the spur leading towards the terminus at Queen's Quay station in August 1950. The spur, which originally terminated outside the station, was authorised originally as a horse tramway in 1888 and extended into the station itself following the electrification of the route in 1905. The track heading north at this point formed the busy route through to Queen's Road. The origins of the station dated back to 1848, when it was opened as the terminus of the Belfast, Holywood & Bangor Railway. Two years later, the Belfast & County Down Railway opened its station alongside the original and, in 1852, the two stations were merged when it became known as Queen's Quay. By the summer of 1950 – following the closure of a number of lines that it served – Queen's Quay was only used by services to and from Bangor. The station was eventually closed on 10 April 1976 following the transfer of services to Belfast Central and was subsequently demolished. The site of the station and its adjacent railway depot – closed in 1994 – has been subsumed within the foundations of the flyover of the M3.

One of the 'DK1' rebuilds – No 78 – is pictured entering the terminal stub that was situated within Queen's Quay station, the terminus of the Belfast & County Down Railway, on 5 June 1948. Although the bulk of the 'DK1' rebuilds came from the batch of 41 cars delivered between 1913 and 1919, nine of the first batch – including No 78 – were also fully rebuilt on 7ft 6in wheelbase trucks between 1929 and 1932. The terminus was last used on 30 October 1953.

It's the end of the shift and huge numbers of workers vacate the factories and yards served by the Queen's Road route to pack on to the many buses and trams waiting to ferry them home. Closest to the camera is Daimler CVA6 No 249; fitted with a Harkness/Park Royal 54-seat body, this was one of a batch of 40 buses delivered during 1947 and was to survive in service until April 1964. Behind, with a service to Crumlin Road, is 'DK1' rebuild No 287 with a 'McCreary' car in the background. The route to Queen's Road was planned in 1904 but not opened until 11 August 1908. By the time that the route opened, the local shipyards, including Harland & Wolff, employed more than 20,000. All-day services to and from Queen's Road ceased in mid-October 1953, although peak-hour services continued until February 1954, with the number of trams operational being reduced as additional replacement buses entered service.

QUEEN'S ROAD

DUNDONALD ROUTE

The Dundonald route had its origins in a horse tramway that ran along Upper Newtownards Road to a terminus at Knock. This section was converted to electric traction in December 1905. Slightly short of the Knock terminus was the depot; this began as a horse tram depot and was to survive as an operational tram depot until 1946 – some three years after the Dundonald route was converted to trolleybus operation. The extension beyond Knock to Dundonald was opened on 7 July 1924. Here a 'Standard Red' is seen at the original Knock terminus. Trolleybuses replaced trams on the Dundonald via Queen's Bridge route on 16 November 1942 and on the service via Albert Bridge on the following 8 March.

BLOOMFIELD

With 'Standard Red' No 173 in the background, 'Moffett' No 295 stands at the Bloomfield terminus on 27 March 1946. By this date, tram operation of the route was entering its final few weeks – the route was converted to trolleybus operation on 5 May 1946 (the first post-war conversion) – and evidence of the imminent alteration can be seen in the presence of the trolleybus turning circle. By this date the Bloomfield route was the final passenger tramway service to use Albert Bridge. The Bloomfield route, which opened on 29 January 1913, connected into the existing route along Woodstock Road (on the route towards Cregagh) before turning left into Beersbridge Road. The route then turned right into Castlereagh Road for a short distance before heading left on the continuation of Beersbridge Road to reach Bloomfield Road. The brick-built structure to the left of the trams was a communal air raid shelter.

ORMEAU ROAD

Ormeau Road was the terminus for two routes: the 15 that entered the city centre via Cromac Street and the 16 that headed via University Avenue and Botanic Avenue to reach Great Victoria Street. The opening of the route along Cromac Street resulted in the system's first abandonment with the closure of the section along Ormeau Avenue in 1912. Pictured at the terminus is 'Moffett' No 340 – prior to the abandonment of the Ravenhill Road service (on 5 September 1940), alternate cars on the route terminated at Ormeau Road as well. Route 16 was diverted on 5 January 1945 as a result of sewer repair work on Botanic Avenue; the section was never reinstated. The Ormeau Road services were abandoned in favour of trolleybuses on 19 April 1948.

STRANMILLIS

Pictured at the Stranmillis terminus on 5 June 1948 is 'Chamberlain' No 347. When the route along Stranmillis Road was originally electrified in 1905, the service terminated at Ridgeway Street (where the horse tramway route had terminated); the extension to the terminus illustrated here was originally proposed in 1909 and opened in 1913. The route was converted to bus operation on 30 July 1951. Prior to conversion, the Stranmillis service had been linked with the service to Queen's Road; thereafter, the latter route was linked to Springfield Road.

The Malone Road route terminated at the junction with Malone Park and, recorded at the terminus, is 'Moffett' No 330. Although undated, the view can be assumed to be post-war, as the tram evinces traces of the modifications for the blackout – the white painted collision fenders and the headlamp shield (designed to minimise illumination during the blackout) – whilst the traction columns retain a white painted band, a further aid to travellers during the blackout. The Malone Road route had its origins in a horse route opened in 1900 that was converted to electric traction in 1905. Linked, when recorded here, as part of a cross-city service to Ballygomartin, the Malone Road section was converted to bus operation on 5 November 1951. In 1920 there were proposals, never completed, for the extension of the route to Rosemary Park, a distance of about half a mile.

An inbound service from Balmoral heads north along Lisburn Road as it passes the junction with Tate's Avenue on 5 June 1948. 'Standard Red' No 153 was not one of the batch to be rebuilt as fully enclosed but the photographer has recorded it as having been equipped with the longer – 7ft 6in wheelbase – truck as used on the 'DK1' rebuilds; a small number of the 'Standard Reds' were so modified without undergoing the full rebuild. Although the property immediately to the left of the tram is still extant and allows for the location to be readily identified, not only has the branch of the Northern Bank closed, the building has been demolished; the unattractive modern building erected on the site is itself empty and vandalised at the time of writing.

No 327 awaits departure from the terminus at Balmoral with an inbound service; although the date of the photograph is unrecorded, it must be towards the end of the route's life, as No 327 carries the post-1951 route number. The Balmoral route was one of the services converted to electric traction during 1905 and the service terminated at the city boundary. The 50 'Moffett' cars – Nos 292-341 – were all built by Brush and were delivered during late 1920 and mid-1921. Originally, all were fitted with Brush-built Brill-type four-wheel trucks of a 7ft 6in wheelbase and subsequently re-equipped with Maley & Taunton 8ft 0in swing link trucks, with the original Brush trucks being reused in the rebuilding of older trams. All of the 'Moffett' cars were scrapped following withdrawal between 1951 and 1953. The Balmoral service was converted on 9 November 1952.

Recorded outside Celtic Park, the home of Belfast Celtic FC, is 'Standard Red' No 49. The Donegall Road route, which terminated just short of the junction with Falls Road, was one of the sections proposed in 1909 and opened on 28 January 1913. The Donegall Road routes were relatively early casualties post-war, being converted to bus operation on 20 April 1947. Belfast Celtic FC was not to survive the tram route by long; in controversial circumstances it withdrew from the Irish League, playing its last league game at Celtic Park on 21 April 1949. The club had originally been established in 1891, with Celtic Park being first used later in the decade. Apart from football, the ground also accommodated greyhound racing and thus survived until October 1983, when the last race meeting was held. The site is now occupied by a shopping centre.

SPRINGFIELD

Two trams stand at the crossover situated at the junction of Springfield Road and Springfield Crescent. Closest to the camera is 'DK1' rebuild No 285, with the conductor having just completed swinging the trolleypole. Both trams have terminated just short of the final terminus, which is about a third of a mile further west round the corner. The two cars had been operating peak-hour services – these had continued to Springfield Road to and from Queen's Road until the summer of 1953 despite the loss of the all-day service (and this view is taken towards the end of this period) – and No 285 is about to return to Mountpottinger depot at the end of its turn. Although C&C Motor Works of 218 Springfield Road no longer exists and the site has been redeveloped, the location can be identified by the distinctive gable end of the house at the end of Springfield Terrace, which is still extant, as is much of the housing on the right-hand side. Pedestrians now have the benefit of a pelican crossing of the main road at this point.

A busy scene at the Springfield terminus, just short of Clovelly Street, sees 'Moffett' No 300 alongside 'Chamberlain' No 369 in August 1951, a year before the Springfield service was converted (on 9 November 1952). Note the conductor on the extreme right; he is equipped with an Ultimate ticket machine, which had only been introduced to Belfast earlier in 1951 and so was a recent addition to the conductor's equipment. This view is unrecognisable today, as the factory to the left has been demolished and the road improved. Springfield Road was one of the routes on which electric trams were introduced on 30 November 1905; its origins lay in a horse tramway route constructed originally in 1899.

BALLYGOMARTIN

With the Woodvale Presbyterian Church in the background, this view of the junction of Ballygomartin Road with Woodvale Road sees 'Moffett' No 329 emerging onto the main road with a service on route 58 from Ballygomartin to Balmoral whilst, in the background, a second car picks up passengers with a service towards Ligoniel on route 56. The 700-yard extension from the junction here to Ballygomartin opened on 23 July 1925; this was to be the final tramway extension opened in the city.

Trams of two generations and two different liveries stand at the terminus at Ballygomartin – Forthriver Road – on 12 June 1948. On the left is No 120; this was one of the original batch of 170 trams delivered in 1905 for the introduction of electric services. Originally open-top, these trams were built by Brush of Loughborough and were fitted with Brill 21E four-wheel trucks; each car cost £586 when new. Known as 'Standard Reds' as a result of the livery carried, all were equipped with open-balcony top covers within a short period and the majority were to retain their open balconies until withdrawal. On the right is 'McCreary' No 420 in Prussian Blue and white; this livery had been adopted by William Chamberlain following his appointment in 1929 as part of his policy to create a new image for the tramway system. Only new cars built after that date or those trams rebuilt were to carry this new livery; unmodernised trams – such as No 120 – retained the red livery throughout their operational lives. The route was one of those routes converted on 10 November 1952.

LIGONIEL ROUTE

Services to Ligoniel could head west out of the city centre along either the Shankill Road and Woodvale Road or the Crumlin Road before completing their journey on the latter from Ardoyne. Recorded prior to heading inbound at Ardoyne in August 1951 is 'Chamberlain' No 349; judging by the lack of passengers, this car has just come out of Ardoyne depot, which was accessed by the tracks heading off to the right behind the tram, and a car emerging from the depot can be seen on the extreme right. In the distance, 'Moffett' No 336 is heading inbound from Ligoniel. Ardoyne depot dated to 1912 and was one of two – the other being Mountpottinger – that retained an allocation of trams through to the system's final closure.

'Chamberlain' No 380 is pictured descending Crumlin Road, at its junction with Glenbank Place, with an inbound service on route 60 towards Balmoral. The section of line from Brookfield Street to St Mark's Church in Ligoniel had originally been promoted by the Belfast & Ligoniel Tramway Co, which had been established in 1892 and which had been authorised by an Order in Council on 25 November 1892. The 1½-mile route opened on 24 April 1893 and was operated from the outset, by agreement, by the Belfast Street Tramways Co. The agreement also gave the BST the right to purchase the Belfast & Ligoniel; this right was exercised in 1902. The route to St Mark's was one of the services electrified by the end of 1905.

In 1913 the terminus of the Ligoniel route was extended a short distance – about half a mile – from the original terminus at St Mark's Church up Ligoniel Road to Mill Avenue. This narrow – but level – street was approached via a hump-backed curve and, in August 1951, 'Chamberlain' No 385 is pictured ascending the hump as it enters Ligoniel Road from Mill Avenue with a service on route 61 towards Balmoral. The steepness of Ligoniel Road at this point can be fully appreciated on the right. This view also shows to good effect the impact of the two-foot rule – whereby the tramway operator was responsible for the maintenance of the public highway to a distance of two feet beyond the outer rail – as the limit is clearly delineated by a string of cobbles parallel to the track. The services to Ligoniel were amongst the last in the city to have an all-day tram service; these were withdrawn on 12 October 1953. Thereafter, the final conversion in February 1954, tram operation over the route was restricted to peak hours only and even this grew less frequent as more replacement buses entered service.

CLIFTONVILLE

The route to Cliftonville was originally one of the last horse tram routes to be opened – in late 1900 – and was to be electrified from 5 December 1905. Pictured at the terminus in July 1946 is No 89; this unique rebuild of a 'Standard Red', which acquired the nickname 'hen house' (or 'Queen Mary'), was undertaken in 1923 to the design of the then rolling stock engineer and was completed in the period between Moffett's departure as general manager and the appointment of Samuel Carlisle. A second route to Cliftonville via Old Park Road was opened in 1913; the original route terminated at a crossover just before the junction with Oldpark Road and the track to the left of No 89 led to the newer terminus. The Cliftonville Road route was converted to bus operation on 31 August 1947 whilst the Oldpark Road route was converted to bus on 30 April 1951; the Ciftonville route was converted to trolleybus operation and extended to the Carr's Glen housing estate at the same time.

Following the acquisition of the Cavehill & Whitewell route in 1911, the corporation also took over eight of the company's fleet of 10 trams; the other two were sold the following year to the Mansfield & District Light Railway Co. Of the eight cars, five were Nos 1-5, which were small cars (fitted with Brill four-wheel trucks), whilst three were larger cars from the batch Nos 6-10; these eight cars became Nos 193-200. However, the larger cars – with their Brush Conaty radial four-wheel trucks – proved unsuitable and so two were rebuilt as 'Standard' 28ft cars and one was scrapped. Eventually, all of the surviving seven were rebuilt as 'Standard' cars and it is in this guise that No 197 is pictured here shortly after the end of World War II.

CREDITS

Lost Tramways of Ireland – Belfast. Published in Great Britain in 2021 by Graffeg Limited.

Written by Peter Waller copyright © 2021. Designed and produced by Graffeg Limited copyright © 2021.

Graffeg Limited, 24 Stradey Park Business Centre, Mwrwg Road, Llangennech, Llanelli, Carmarthenshire, SA14 8YP, Wales, UK. Tel: 01554 824000. www.graffeg.com.

Peter Waller is hereby identified as the author of this work in accordance with section 77 of the Copyrights, Designs and Patents Act 1988.

A CIP Catalogue record for this book is available from the British Library.

ISBN 9781914079504

1 2 3 4 5 6 7 8 9

MIX
Paper from responsible sources
FSC
www.fsc.org   FSC® C014138

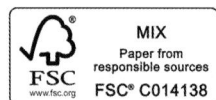

Photo credits

© Barry Cross Collection/Online Transport Archive: pages 15, 16, 19, 44.
© C. Carter: pages 20, 50.
© R. W. A. Jones/Online Transport Archive: pages 21, 22, 24, 26, 30, 31, 32, 33, 41, 43, 52, 54, 55, 56, 58, 60, 61.
© Martin Jenkins Collection/Online Transport Archive: page 27.
© J. Joyce Collection/Online Transport Archive: pages 29, 49.
© John Meredith/Online Transport Archive: pages 34, 36, 40, 42, 47, 51, 57.
© F. N. T. Lloyd-Jones/Online Transport Archive: pages 35, 46, 63.
© W. A. Camwell/National Tramway Museum: page 38.
© Des Coakham, courtesy Andy Crockart and Derek Young: pages 45, 62.
© Scottish Tramway & Transport Society: page 53.

The photographs used in this book have come from a variety of sources. Wherever possible contributors have been identified although some images may have been used without credit or acknowledgement and if this is the case apologies are offered and full credit will be given in any future edition.

Lost Tramways of Wales:

- **Cardiff** ISBN 9781912213122
- **North Wales** ISBN 9781912213139
- **South Wales and Valleys** ISBN 9781912213146
- **Swansea and Mumbles** ISBN 9781912213153

Lost Tramways of England:

- **Birmingham North** ISBN 9781912654390
- **Birmingham South** ISBN 9781912654383
- **Bradford** ISBN 9781912654406
- **Brighton** ISBN 9781912654376
- **Bristol** ISBN 9781912654345
- **Coventry** ISBN 9781912654338
- **Leeds West** ISBN 9781913733506
- **Leeds East** ISBN 9781914079580
- **Nottingham** ISBN 9781912654352
- **Southampton** ISBN 9781912654369

Lost Tramways of Scotland:

- **Aberdeen** ISBN 9781912654413
- **Dundee** ISBN 9781912654420
- **Edinburgh** ISBN 9781913733513
- **Glasgow South** ISBN 9781914079528
- **Glasgow North** ISBN 9781914079542

Lost Tramways of Ireland:

- **Belfast** ISBN 9781914079504